MAKING
MIDCENTURY
MODERN

MAKING MIDCENTURY MODERN

CHRISTOPHER KENNEDY

Photography by **J. Rockwell Seebach**

Foreword by **Barclay Butera**

GIBBS SMITH
TO ENRICH AND INSPIRE HUMANKIND

21   5 4

Copyright © 2017 by Christopher Kennedy
Photographs © 2017 by J. Rockwell Seebach,
except pages 12–13 © Lance Gerber,
pages x, 3, 4, 194–195 © Grey Crawford

Published by
Gibbs Smith
P.O. Box 667
Layton, Utah 84041

1.800.835.4993 orders
www.gibbs–smith.com

Designed by Sheryl Dickert
Printed and bound in China

Gibbs Smith books are printed on either recycled, 100% post–
consumer waste, FSC–certified papers or on paper produced
from sustainable PEFC–certified forest/controlled wood source.
Learn more at www.pefc.org.

Library of Congress Cataloging–in–Publication Data

Names: Kennedy, Christopher, author.
Title: Making midcentury modern / Christopher Kennedy ;
photographs by J. Rockwell Seebach; foreword by Barclay
Butera.
Description: First edition. | Layton, Utah : Gibbs Smith, 2017.
Identifiers: LCCN 2016031422 | ISBN 9781423646495
Subjects: LCSH: Kennedy, Christopher––Themes, motives. |
Interior
   decoration––United States. | Midcentury modern
(Architecture)––United States.
Classification: LCC NK2004.3 .K46 2017 | DDC 747.0973––dc23
LC record available at https://lccn.loc.gov/2016031422
ISBN 13: 978–1–4236–4649–5

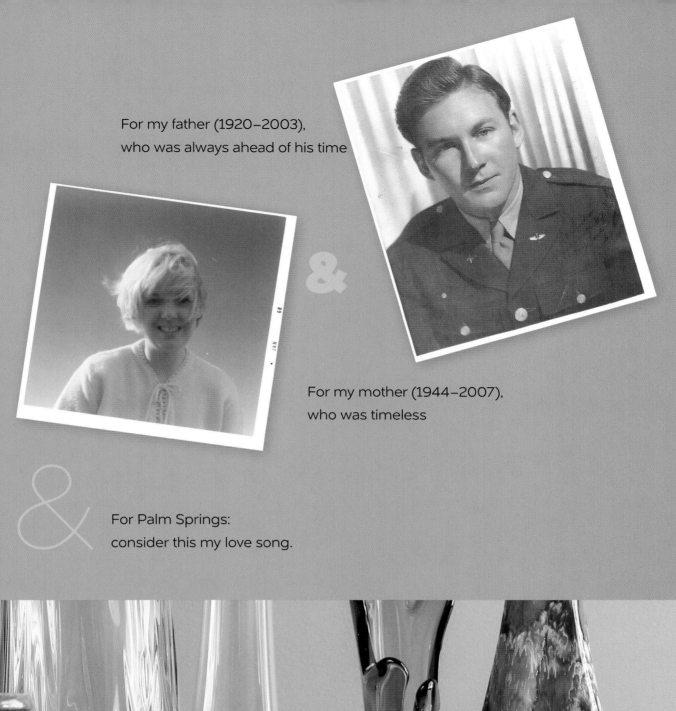

For my father (1920–2003),
who was always ahead of his time

&

For my mother (1944–2007),
who was timeless

&

For Palm Springs:
consider this my love song.

FOREWORD

Working from his base in Palm Springs, Christopher Kennedy's name has become synonymous with midcentury California glamour. His work with modernism has catapulted the design medium to the forefront of our community's consciousness. He's taken a venue that is often misinterpreted and simplified the process of creating midcentury design in the home with his clear vision.

Having had the opportunity to work with Christopher, he has become a great friend and colleague of mine. He and I share a deep-seated passion for couture and the great fashion houses of Europe, and it's through our love of this medium that we both find incredible joy and the heart of our creativity within our design work.

It's a tremendous thrill and an honor to have been asked to write this foreword. Christopher is a man with incredible vision who is extremely confident and accomplished. I predict that you'll find some inspiration here to spark your own creativity.

Barclay Butera

INTRODUCTION

I believe in traditions. I believe in rituals of hearth and home. I believe in chopping vegetables, wrapping presents, and setting the table.

Call me sentimental.

I miss the days when people got dressed to go on airplanes—or even just for dinner. I miss the time when families sat down to dine together; when people would talk and not just text; when kids would stay outside and ride their bikes until sundown; when our country was less fractured; when common courtesy was, well, common.

My mother, Marilyn, was a social worker. She taught me to send handwritten thank you notes and to make my bed each day. She taught me how to dress and to make a good first impression. She taught me that kindness is free and that a smile is always in style.

My father, Robert, was an entrepreneur; a semi-pro boxer, and a soldier in World War II. He taught me to take the road less traveled. He taught me to take care of my possessions. He taught me to live each day to the fullest, to always keep my car clean, and to approach life as a grand adventure.

I do my best to honor their legacy, and as I look at the work on these pages—my unfolding life's work—it becomes evident that I am decidedly nostalgic. But I don't feel that I am nostalgic for a certain architect, a certain form, or a certain chair. Rather, I am nostalgic for that simpler, more gracious time. I think that we as a society have a similar collective yearning.

Perhaps that is why midcentury modern design has had, and continues to have, a hold on the American consciousness. From television shows, to car commercials, to the fashion runway, what many critics have called a "trend" seems to have no indication of slowing down any time soon.

Yet not all of us can live in a pedigreed midcentury modern home. Fear not; the principles of midcentury modern design can be applied to the most unassuming of dwellings. The midcentury modernists were creating a movement that eschewed excess and needless ornament, so if your abode is humble, there is no reason to worry. I choose small and well-appointed over wanton grandeur any day.

This book is intended to help you create a midcentury modern look by offering foolproof tips for introducing modernist design into your home.

This book is also intended to help you make midcentury *modern*. In all of my interior designs, I strive to incorporate the principles of midcentury modernism in a way that feels fresh, relevant, and current. I never want my clients to feel as if they are living in a museum or time capsule.

Because I believe that nostalgia—and design, for that matter—is much more than skin deep, you will notice that much of my advice is dedicated to the life behind the style.

The celebrated midcentury designers were decidedly forward-thinking. They were using the new technology of the time (plastic, fiberglass, bent wood) and creating shapes that had never been seen before. They were dreamers and futurists. I like to think that if they were alive today, they would be creating "what's new" and not resting on their sixty-year-old laurels. I feel that the best way to honor the legacy of these masters is to incorporate their pieces into designs that are decidedly of this century.

So, welcome, and enjoy. Design; create; dream. The past is our muse and the future our canvas.

1 MAKE AN ENTRANCE

We love our colorful doors in Palm Springs. It's not uncommon to see orange doors, pink doors, green doors. . . . Even if you don't live in a modernist post-and-beam home, why not have some fun with your first impression? (Don't forget, black or very dark brown can make a great statement too. Paired with chrome or bronze, it will provide a bold and tailored first look.)

At our home in Palm Springs, we installed marble tile in a striking black-and-white pattern, paired it with a vintage light found at a flea market, and painted the door a high-gloss turquoise. Hello, gorgeous!

2 DRESS THE PART

Call me old-fashioned, but I miss the days when people dressed up. When men wore hats, women wore dresses, and everyone had a certain sense of decorum. I still believe in dressing for the theater and for travel. I'm tired of getting on airplanes alongside people wearing their pajamas.

It doesn't need to be about vanity. For me, dressing the part is about putting your best foot forward; it's about feeling good about yourself and setting positive intentions for your day. Dressing your best is not just a sign of respect for yourself but also for the people around you. Boys, pull up your pants! Girls, leave a little something to the imagination. And remember: good clothes open all doors.

3 MAKE YOUR BED

I believe in making one's bed every day and making it easy to do so. This simple ritual makes me feel as if my life—or at least that small part of it—is in order. What's more, it is so much nicer to crawl into a made bed after a long day.

In our busy modern world, I keep my bedding simple, striking, and foolproof. All you need are sheets, pillows, coverlet, duvet, and one or two decorative pillows.

MY SECRET TO A BEAUTIFUL AND EASY-TO-MAKE BED

STEP 1: *Pull the top sheet all the way up.*

STEP 2: *Pull the coverlet (I prefer one in a fun or contrasting color) all the way up, hiding the wrinkly sheets.*

STEP 3: *Pull the duvet up, but then turn it down in half or thirds at the foot of the bed.*

STEP 4: *Stack the sleeping pillows (David and I like two each) on top of the coverlet.*

STEP 5: *Toss the decorative pillow(s) in front of the sleeping pillows. I often opt for just one large lumbar pillow. I never laden a bed with dozens of pillows that need to be thrown off each night, then rearranged each morning—too much work!*

{ **CK SECRET**

Don't have much room for bedside tables? Free up surface space by hanging your bedside lights.

5

4

EAT BREAKFAST

Do not skip this important meal.

It feeds your body *and* soul.

Gather your thoughts, boost

your metabolism, and set your

daily intentions before venturing

out into the world.

THE COMPLETE
COOKIE JAR

tea

flour   sugar

5 LET PHOTOS TELL YOUR STORY

As much as I love vintage celebrity photographs, or those by Slim Aarons—and I do—lately I have been surrounding myself with family photographs. What better way to channel the joie de vivre of your mid–century predecessors than by letting them smile upon you? And don't think you need to relegate the photos to a hallway or dusty album. In my kitchen, I placed a photograph of my aunt (and godmother), Audrey, on the open shelf where I keep my everyday china. Her beauty and style inspire me daily.

Isn't my auntie beautiful? The Snoopy and Woodstock shakers are relics from my childhood. Why keep such treasures packed away? They remind me of where I come from.

6 SPEAK ITALIAN

When it comes to sofas—the workhorses of the room—I favor modern and new. Vintage upholstery tends to be out of scale for our contemporary homes (and bodies!).

To keep things fresh and comfortable, my trick is to mix Italian modern upholstery with vintage lamps, chairs, and tables for a blend that is simultaneously now and totally timeless.

My colleague's Boston Terrier, Dolly, strikes a pose at my home in Palm Springs. It is not essential that your furry family members match your décor, but it helps.

ANDY WARHOL
Polaroids 1958–1987

11

7 BRASS IS BACK

For some of us, it never left. Few other metals allow for the detail, warmth, and patina the way that brass does. I'm not a purist when it comes to metals—mix and match throughout your home!

Caveat, modernista: I tend to keep my door and plumbing hardware consistent throughout the home, but then get adventurous when it comes to lighting and accessories.

8 FILTER YOUR VIEW

As modern floor plans became more open, thanks to post–and–beam construction, architects got creative with room dividers. Many a midcentury manse featured a carved wood screen, functionally dividing the space while allowing light and breezes to pass through.

At my home in Palm Springs, I used a Don Harvey *brise–soleil* (French for "break the sun") salvaged from the exterior of a medical building in Boulder, Colorado, to separate my dining and living rooms.

9

A FINE BALANCE

One of the most recognizable designs of the era, tension lamps were created to go from the floor to a standard eight-foot ceiling. They still work in most contemporary homes, drawing the eye upward and illuminating dark corners with nostalgic flair. It is time to bring this mid-mod classic out of retirement!

I picked up this handsome lamp for less than $100 at a thrift store; it strikes an instant mid-mod note in my otherwise modern den.

10 BUTT OUT

I have never smoked a cigarette in my life, but I collect vintage ashtrays. The artistry is often incredible, so I use them to gather my personal effects. It lets me feel as cool as Don Draper, with none of the nasty side effects.

11 GO FOR THE GOLD

Silver, chrome, and brushed nickel are all the rage in today's contemporary interiors. Why not add some vintage glamour with the king of all metals?

12 **GO POSTAL**

A midcentury mindset can start curbside. Tell the world you appreciate the days of snail mail, landlines, and casseroles by swapping out your mundane mailbox for this stylish one from Modbox.

13 LAMP UP

Vintage lamps are undoubtedly my favorite item to shop for. A good vintage lamp will instantly change the feel of the most ho–hum room.

{ **CK SECRET**
Online websites like Etsy and Chairish are treasure troves of single vintage lamps, many of which cost less than $100.

14 ORANGE YOU GLAD?

Few colors pack the punch of orange. It is the caffeine of the color wheel. A small (or large) dose of the hue is sure to put a smile on your face and pep in your step.

15 BE BOLD

It is no secret that I like things crisp, graphic, and bright. Modern artwork is my preferred method to place a midcentury–inspired interior decid–edly in this century. A punch of geo–metric pow paired with vintage furnishings just stirs my soul. Go bold or go home!

16 CHANNEL YOUR INNER LUCY AND RICKY

Two beds were *de rigueur* for midcentury married couples, or at least those on TV! Who can forget Lucy and Ricky Ricardo, or June and Ward Cleaver, in their separate beds?

Many of the homes I design incorporate at least one guest room with twin beds. It's a practical way to accommodate family and friends, and the symmetry looks quite smashing.

In this guest room, I created one long wall-size headboard. While the room is often used for children, when a couple comes to stay, the mattresses are easily pushed together and topped with a featherbed. Snuggle away!

29

(NEUTRA)FACE IT

I have this thing with fonts. It is a bit of a problem. Typeface sets the tone, so make your home address ring modern with the king of all lettering: Neutraface. Created by the architect Richard Neutra, his numerals are available online and will instantly enhance the curb appeal of the most humble abode.

18 EMBRACE THE OLD AND THE NEW

The midcentury masters were pushing the envelope of technology and innovation. In a few short decades, we now have more technology in the palm of our hand than they could have dreamt about. In this modern age, why not surround yourself with some well-chosen midcentury nostalgia? It is a wonderful reminder of where we have come from and a nudge at where we have yet to go. So dream on, modernista! The world is literally at your fingertips.

19

BURN BRIGHT

I've seen maudlin brick or stone fireplaces in many homes from a variety of periods, including my parents' 1970s rancher. A coat of white paint is an affordable and foolproof trick to add midcentury appeal to any hearth.

Here, the crushed glass adds a dash of millenium modernity to an otherwise vintage vibe.

20 STAR GAZE

I like to avoid cliché, but I am all about icons. The "Sputnik" chandelier—named after the Soviet Union's 1957 satellite, which launched the space race and the "atomic age" of design—always casts a heavenly glow.

PATTERN PLAY

Pile on the pattern! Mix some modern geometry with vintage fabrics for a look that is at once retro-chic and of-the-moment. In this case, more really is more.

22 LIFE IS BEAUTIFUL

For this client's home, we tracked down *Life* magazines from the year the house was built. No matter the age of your home, vintage magazines will take you back to a simpler, more gracious time.

Have a new or new-ish house? Consider buying vintage magazines (easily found online) from the year you were born—or the year you wish you were.

23 CAN IT

Add instant flair to your kitchen with a set of vintage canisters. I happen to use my mother's. Don't do much baking? Get creative! They are equally suited to storing packets of sweetener, straws, protein powder, and K–Cups® (in my kitchen, anyway!).

24 SHADY DEALS

Midcentury masters were all about the details. They left no design stone unturned, including one that is often overlooked—the humble lampshade. Today's boring white diffusers just lack the luster of their predecessors, which often featured tassels, decorative tape trim, or bold colors.

Get creative, dear modernist! Swap out a standard shade for a deep color. Buy some tape trim, break out the glue gun, and let there be light.

Palm Springs Paradise Moruzzi

25 GO EXOTIC

With the advent of commercial air travel, a certain wanderlust took hold of many mid–century Americans. As they ventured to far flung locales, or dreamt of doing so, all sorts of exotica made its way into American interior design. Even if you won't be visiting Palm Springs anytime soon, incorporating tropical décor into your home can transform your bedroom into your favorite hotel suite.

The Beverly Hills Hotel and Blanche Devereaux's bedroom have nothing on this wallpaper from my friends at Phillip Jeffries.

26

GET SKIN IN THE GAME

Cowhide rugs have been a staple of modern decorating since before the midcentury era. Eileen Gray, designer of her eponymous chrome and glass circular side table, famously decorated her apartment with them back in the 1930s. I like to use cowhide rugs in spaces that are difficult to fit a standard rectangular area rug, such as this entryway.

27 MAKE A WISH

Danish designer Hans Wegner, an icon of "organic functionality," designed more than five hundred chairs in his lifetime, but few remain as relevant today as his 1949 Wishbone Chair. I paired Wegner's chairs with a traditional trestle table and Jonathan Adler chandelier for a timeless look.

28 LET NATURE BE YOUR GUIDE

Midcentury modern architects were using new technologies and building techniques to enhance our connection to the outside environment. If you don't live in a post-and-beam modern masterpiece, never fear! You can still bring the outdoors in with a nature-inspired color palette. Blues and greens are my go-to decorating colors. With just a dash of sunny yellow, I can practically smell the fresh air and feel the sun on my face.

29 GET SHIPWRECKED

I grew up watching *Gilligan's Island* and *The Love Boat*, and I have sought warm climes ever since. (There is a reason I found my way to Palm Springs!) The idea of getting shipwrecked and spending the rest of one's days on sunny shores has a certain hold on the American psyche. The popularity of the Tiki style and restaurants like Trader Vic's is a testament to this wanderlust. We may not be able to live on Fantasy Island, but a few hours in an easy-to-install hammock will put you in a tropical state of mind.

30 LIGHTEN UP

In many ways, modernism was a backlash against excessive ornamentation and overwrought copy–cat architecture. Modernists were wiping the slate clean. You can do the same by keeping things simple—a crisp white color palette will always give a fresh outlook on life.

Against a bright backdrop, small pops of color make a big statement.

31 METAL-URGE

As midcentury designers experimented with new forms, no material was off limits: wood, fiberglass, acrylic, and metal were all just putty in their hands.

32 LET THE SUNSHINE IN

You do not need to live in Palm Springs to hail the sunshine! A common midcentury decorating theme, these sunbursts came in a variety of forms—wood, metal, and more. A nice counterpoint to canvas artwork, a sunburst is sure to brighten the coldest of winters and add a dash of midcentury optimism to your décor.

33 CLAY-MATION

A close runner-up to glass bottles, midcentury pottery is my second favorite obsession to shop for. They are a bit harder to find but well worth the effort. Group them together for maximum impact. And don't be afraid to put them to use! Add flowers, plants, fruit, whatever you can dream up. Our grandparents valued the utility of everyday objects, not just the beauty.

34 COLOR ME BLUE

True story: Years ago, when my design firm had only been open a short while, the home editor for the *Los Angeles Times* came to Palm Springs looking for projects. I showed her a few homes I had done, and I was over the moon—but a bit incredulous—a few weeks later when she called and said, "I want to publish that blue house."

I said, "I don't like blue. What do you mean?"

Her kind response, "Christopher, apparently you do."

She was correct, of course; nearly every shade of the watery hue was represented in that particular project. To this day, blue is one of my tried-and-true colors. If you want to add a dash of midcentury cool to your home, look no further than blue and its sassy cousins aqua and turquoise.

35 TAKE IT OUTSIDE

A primary tenet of midcentury architecture was to create a connection to the environment. One of the first and greatest modern houses, Philip Johnson's Glass House (1949), was a glass box dropped into the Connecticut landscape. Given the climate, the connection was largely visual. When the principles of modernism moved west to warmer temperatures, the great architects worked to make those glass walls movable, to create a physical connection to the environment.

No matter where you live, even if only for a month or two in the summer, take it outside! Create an outdoor living room with rugs, pillows, artwork, and all the creature comforts of your indoor rooms. You will find that you create some of your happiest memories in the *plein air.*

IT *IS* EASY BEING GREEN

The optimism of Kermit the Frog, the magic of chlorophyll, the aroma of fresh-cut grass—green's got it all going on.

My Giselle chairs flank a vintage sideboard adorned with an eclectic mix of decorative objects.

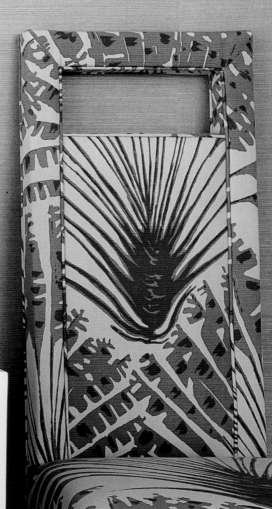

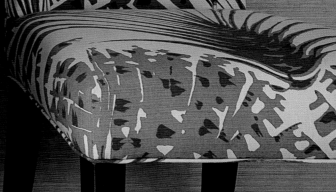

37
AFRICAN RHYTHM

March to the beat of a different drum. Mask your insecurities. Walk on the wild side. Dream of far–flung locales and wild safaris. A dash of Africana in your home can take you places you never thought you could go.

38 THROW A CURVE BALL

Every yin needs a yang. Hot needs cold.
Darkness cannot exist without light.
While midcentury design is known for
its clean, straight lines, they are only
enhanced by the unexpected addition
of a sinuous curve.

Architect Frank Gehry's iconic Wiggle Chair (1972) is a perfect
complement to a metal desk and Phillip Jeffries grasscloth.

39 SEND A HANDWRITTEN NOTE

My mother raised me to write thank–you notes. I never enjoyed the chore, but I dutifully wrote them after each birthday and holiday. In an age of electronic communication, paper–and–ink stands out. I can honestly say that handwritten notes are one of the secrets to my success. Thanks, Mom!

{ ## CK SECRET

There are many wonderful online sources, like Zazzle or Moo, that offer personalized stationery. If staying true to midcentury custom: Men, order a single "correspondence card" (no fold) with your name embossed across the top. Ladies, opt for a more decorative folding card, if you prefer.

40 WHITE OUT

My sure-fire tip for bringing a modern touch to any kitchen? White countertops. My preference is natural quartz from Silestone, but Corian or even Formica (that midcentury marvel) will also do the trick.

To set yourself apart, avoid granite—the staple of tract homes and big box builders. A white counter, even when paired with more traditional cabinetry, will provide a breath of fresh air to your kitchen.

41 BLACK & LIGHT

Believe it or not, I am a simple guy. I like things classic. I try not to get tricky with building materials. Marble was a design staple thousands of years ago—and fifty years ago. Who am I to mess with success?

In this Palm Springs living room, black marble edged with brass trim provides a dramatic backdrop for artwork from my client's native South Africa, paired with a sculpture purchased on a trip to Asia. This timeless material of marble, which is also surprisingly affordable, lets my client's collection take center stage.

42 THINK PINK

Pink was arguably *the* color of the 1950s; no doubt you have seen an iconic midcentury pink bathroom. It started with Dorothy Draper in the 1940s and continued with Mamie Eisenhower, who wore a pink gown bejeweled with 2,000 rhinestones to Ike's inauguration in 1953. Pink being her favorite color, Mamie reportedly had the entire White House private quarters decorated in the hue, so it is no surprise that pink soared to popularity in decorating and fashion during the decade.

43

FIRE IT UP

Nothing says "home" like a hearth—be it inside or out. From space-age metal cones to solid stone chimneys, most mid-century homes were centered around a fireplace.

The present-day gas fireplaces, often covered with a thin piece of glass, leave me a bit cold. A roaring fire takes me back: to campgrounds, to holidays, to bedtime stories. Put your smart phone down, pull up a chair, raise a glass, and gather 'round. You will be glad you did.

44
EERO WON'T STEER YOU WRONG

As an interior designer, I spend much of my time selecting furniture. Dining tables, in general, are an item that I frequently agonize over. How many people do my clients need to seat for dinner? Will the finish be durable? Is the scale right for the room?

I really shouldn't fret. Eero Saarinen (who also designed the St. Louis Gateway Arch) created the perfect table several decades ago.

His marble table works in almost every setting. Place this table in a traditional home, and like a fresh breeze on a warm day, it instantly lightens the air. The table easily seats eight, which is almost always plenty. Done in marble, the table is dura–ble and timeless. Its oval shape allows for easy conversation amongst all diners. Bravo, Mr. Saarinen!

CK SECRET

Don't have the budget for the marble table? The fiberglass version is equally versatile. Even IKEA makes a very good option that captures the essence of Eero's original intent.

45 SHOW YOUR ROOTS

For all the clean lines and square corners of midcentury design, there was a simultaneous movement to embrace nature. The great furniture designer George Nakashima experimented with the juxtaposition of live edges and machine precision. Each enhances the other.

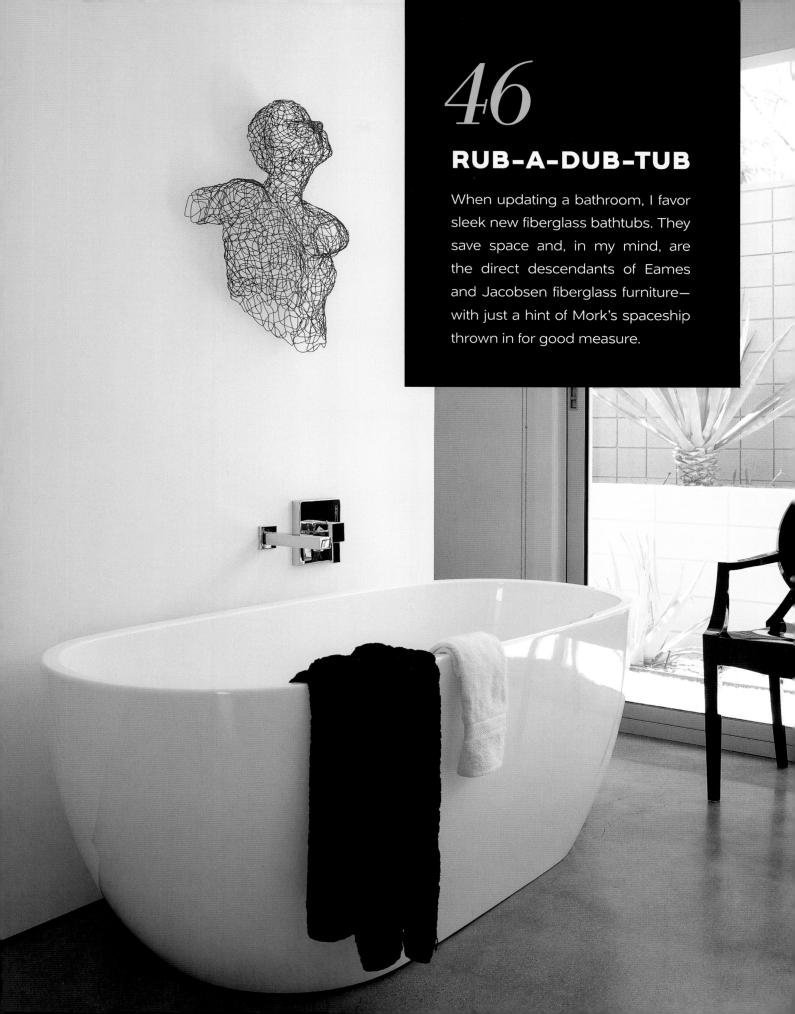

46
RUB-A-DUB-TUB

When updating a bathroom, I favor sleek new fiberglass bathtubs. They save space and, in my mind, are the direct descendants of Eames and Jacobsen fiberglass furniture—with just a hint of Mork's spaceship thrown in for good measure.

47

BLACK, WHITE & RED ALL OVER

From Piet Mondrian to Charles and Rae Eames, iconic designers have known the power of these three colors for nearly a century. While it is admittedly not my favorite color, no other hue packs the punch of red. I turned to this classic color scheme in the living room of the desert retreat I created for a Silicon Valley mogul.

Overleaf: In a nod to my 1970s roots, I topped the room off with a photo mural depicting Joshua Tree National Park.

48

PUT SOME SIZZLE IN YOUR SWIZZLE

My parents collected swizzle sticks from their travels and evenings out. I inherited the tradition, but these supper club relics are becoming increasingly less common. Sentimentalist that I am, I carry these beauties from California Lustre at my shop in Palm Springs. More often, I use them for my coffee. Stir away!

49 FLOWER POWER

Bring some 1960s peace and love into your home with a groovy floral pattern. Flowers are perennial symbols of fleeting beauty and the preciousness of life. Classic Marimekko patterns are a good place to start.

50 SERVE IT UP

Vintage melamine dishware is an affordable and simple way to add some midcentury nostalgia to your entertaining. In addition, melamine is nearly indestructible and comes in every color of the rainbow: Now serving fun!

51

DOWN TO THE WIRE

If you don't live in sunshine year-round, midcentury metal furniture will withstand the colder months. No need to find a complete set—it is more fun to mix and match a variety of outdoor metal styles. A coat of white outdoor spray paint, available off the shelf at your local hardware store, will bring it all together.

52 WAKE UP

Dating back to 1897, the Heywood–Wakefield Company is something of an unsung hero in midcentury design. Their recognizable Art Deco–inspired pieces, often made using steam to bend the wood and a bleaching process to lighten it, have become collector's items.

53 MIX IT UP

Interiors in the middle of the twentieth century didn't just turn Danish modern overnight. Unless you were part of the midcentury 1 percent, it is unlikely that you suddenly transformed your home's decor. Most Americans adopted the new trend slowly, adding a piece here or there. Thus, true midcentury interiors were a mix of more tra-ditional pieces and the emerging modern style.

Louis XIV armchairs mix with a Noguchi-inspired dining table and '70s mod fabric in my eclectic design for this dining room.

54

WALNUT
AND **WHITE**

. . . and everything bright!
No other color combination
captures the midcentury
essence as these two
complementary hues. Like
ebony and ivory, together
they create beautiful music.

55

LESS IS MORE

Pare it down. Let it go. It is just stuff. Most of us have far too many possessions. What do you really need? What moves you? What inspires you? Focus on that, and forget the rest.

56 BLOCK PARTY

I have had a minor obsession with grids since my days in architecture school. It is no wonder that my Franklin credenza draws inspiration from cubist geometry. Throw in a bouffant hairdo and a dry martini, and you had me at "hello."

57 HORSE AROUND

Equine majesty has captured the human imagination for millennia. Grace, strength, loyalty, dignity, hard work—we can learn much from these four-legged companions. I paired a vintage ceramic horse sculpture with a 1960s faux bamboo lamp for a tableau of striking simplicity.

Don't be afraid of the pleated shade!

58

CIRCLE THE WAGONS

Why play it straight? It is so expected. A semicircular sofa invites conversation and sets a retro tone.

BONUS ROUND: Cork floors are both eco–friendly and soft underfoot.

Interested in mid–mod design but don't know where to start? Take a seat, my friend. One good chair can transform a room. They say that a chair is the most difficult piece of furniture to design and if done correctly captures the essence of an entire design movement.

60 PROCURE A PLATNER

Warren Platner (1919–2006) designed one of the most enduring dining sets in the history of interior design. He also created the interiors for the Ford Foundation and the Windows on the World restaurant atop the World Trade Center. Used separately or together, these pieces stand the test of time.

After receiving his degree in architecture from Cornell University in 1941, Platner worked for some of the most renowned architects of the twentieth century, including I. M. Pei, Raymond Loewy, and Eero Saarinen before opening his own firm in 1967.

61 GET STONED

Think Frank Lloyd Wright's Fallingwater and E. Stewart Williams' Frank Sinatra Estate— great midcentury houses were often built around a central stone fireplace. Go for the real deal if you can, but today we have stone veneer to create a *trompe l'oeil* masonry look.

62 FLAT OUT COOL

With cabinetry, beauty is in the simplicity.

No raised paneling for me, no thank you!

Forgo the adornment and let the beauty

of the wood have its moment in the sun.

GO NUTS

It is no secret that walnut is the preferred wood species of midcentury designers. You want a midcentury look? Then get the red out. I tend to avoid any wood finish that appears overly red or orange (with the notable exception of teak).

64 BUTTERFLY EFFECT

The humble Butterfly Chair has a rich lineage: It was first designed in Buenos Aires, Argentina, in 1938 by the architects Antonio Bonet, Juan Kurchan, and Jorge Ferrari Hardoy, who met as assistants in Le Corbusier's Paris studio. (Yes, *that* Le Corbusier!) Their utilitarian seat inspired today's camping chairs, that modern staple of tailgate parties and campouts across the USA. While it does not come with a built-in cup holder, I much prefer the original. Simple, sleek, and affordable, it brings style and sophistication wherever it goes.

65 WIPE YOUR MOUTH

Bring back a bit of midcentury propriety and sophistication with cloth napkins. Vintage collectible linen sets are very affordable and easy to find on the Internet or at flea markets. No need to save them for special occasions—if you can wash your undies, you can wash napkins. They elevate any meal into an event, and the landfill will thank you. As that immortal advertising adage says, "You're worth it."

66 CUT THE GRASS

Afraid of wallpaper? Fear that modern design is too sterile for you? Take the edge off with wallpaper made from bamboo, jute, rush, or sea grass. A staple of midcentury interior design, grasscloth has stood the test of time.

67

SET THE TABLE

There was a time when families sat down to dinner together; when people would talk, not text; when anniversaries and birthday messages were not the domain of social media. Turn the television off and put down the smart phone. Light the candles, break the bread, raise your glass. Life is a series of golden moments, every day and in every way. So set the table; get out the good china. Why not tonight?

68 FRESH COAT

A simple and surefire way to give your home a modern face-lift is with a coat of white paint. White was the go-to color of modernist architects, starting in the 1920s with the Bauhaus and International styles. White offers purity of expression in architectural design while enhancing the play of light and shadow.

69 "TERR" IT UP

Originally invented by the Venetians (so you know it's good), terrazzo flooring is poured in place and composed of scraps of quartz, marble, granite, and/or glass held together with a polymer resin. Many of us grew up with terrazzo floors in our elementary schools and department stores, so the material continues to have nostalgic appeal. Why not use terrazzo technology in a modern way, on your kitchen counters? Composed of 100 percent post-consumer recycled glass, these slabs from Vetrazzo are both beautiful and eco-friendly.

70 DINE IN

From Arnold's on *Happy Days* to Mel's Diner on *Alice* and The Peach Pit on *90210*, many life moments have been immortalized at a small-screen diner. Set the stage for your life by turning a cramped nook into a diner-inspired eating space with banquette seating.

Your booth seating does not need to be custom. A local discount home store will carry leather benches; push them against the wall and pile on some throw pillows to create your version of the classic American diner. Ding, ding—order's up!

71 TAKE THE PLUNGE

If you love something, go for it. Dive in, feet first. Especially when it comes to your interior. If you love something the first time you see it, chances are you will love it the thousandth time. The great midcentury designers were not timid; they were brave. They put themselves out there. They took risks—and it paid off.

In this small powder room, I embraced the dark space and my client's love of the sea to create a magical and immersive experience.

SHAG, BABY!

Technically dating from the 1970s (much like myself), shag carpeting has nonetheless become synonymous with today's midcentury-inspired interior. A shag rug, be it synthetic or the more natural flokati style, is my preferred floor covering to unify an eclectic interior.

73

BE BRUTALLY HONEST

A descendant of International Style modernism, Brutalism in architecture dates from the 1950s to the 1970s. Brutalist décor elements favored raw–edge metal or concrete and reached their heyday in the 1970s. Think *American Hustle,* not *Grease,* and you will get the idea. Warning, dear mod–ernist: as with many good things, a little can go a long way.

74 ASK TRINA

There may be no singular, simpler gesture to bringing midcentury joie de vivre into your space than accenting with Trina Turk pillows. The queen of retro sunny California fashion, just one pillow from Trina's home goods line will brighten your day. In multiples, you may need to wear shades.

75

BUY A BAR CART

No built-in wet bar? No problem! A staple of midcentury décor, a bar cart can turn any unused corner into happy hour. You will practically be able to hear Dean Martin crooning on the hi-fi.

76 BOX IT UP

From Cubism in art to Eames–era modular furniture, simple cubby shelving has a proud lineage. No need to relegate them to children's rooms and IKEA warehouses! These geometric goodies will give you a place for everything and keep everything in its place, while adding architectural rigor to your décor.

BOTTOMS UP!

In Palm Springs, we have our cocktail culture down to a science. No matter where you live, add some swank to your mixology with a set of vintage glassware.

78

EXPRESS YOURSELF

Midcentury stoicism is one nostalgic principle to which I do not ascribe. Let it out: laugh, cry, scream, sing. Emotions are the voice of the soul. Let it be heard and let your home reflect who you are.

Do you ever feel like the woman in Nina Fowler's *Wild Ride?* We all do, sometimes! Let it out. It is the best way to move on.

79 TOP SHELF

Midcentury designers were masters of form and function, finding solutions that were elegant in their simplicity. I increased the function of this compact kitchen by adding three floating shelves to the existing cabinetry design. They keep everyday dishware at arm's reach while injecting color into the space; the black faux crocodile wallpaper adds a dose of depth and drama.

80

ATOM BOMB

From cellular biology to outer space, great minds of the mid–twentieth century began to explore every part of our incredible world. Bring a bit of that scientific curiosity home with molecule-inspired furniture and an out–of–this–world color palette.

81

I CAN'T DO THAT, DAVE

Few household items are decidedly less midcentury than our (wonderful) big-screen televisions. These modern marvels are more "HAL 9000" than 1968. Midcentury televisions were often incorporated into pleasing pieces of casegoods. In that tradition, I try to camouflage flat-screens by placing them against a dark wall (wood paneling, paint, or wallpaper are all good options), minimizing their looming presence. Bonus: the deep background color is easier on the eyes when viewing your favorite show.

82 GRANDMA KNOWS BEST

Floral patterns were really quite common in 1950s and 1960s interiors but are often left out of the textbooks and overshadowed by innovations of the era. For those who worry that modernism might be too masculine for your taste, you're in luck: "Granny florals" are making a comeback.

I tempered the bold geometry of this bedroom with an oversize floral print from Designers Guild.

83 MIXED MESSAGES

One of the design questions I am asked most often is, "Can I mix metals in my home?" My answer is a resounding, "Yes!" Most of my clients opt for chrome or nickel fixtures but don't hesitate to mix in brass or gold accents, like this vintage mirror in an otherwise modern bathroom.

84 BE A BARBIE GIRL

Launched in 1959 by Mattel, Barbie® is a true midcentury icon. But don't let your beauty be only skin deep, my modern friend. True allure requires both style and substance.

85 HANG OUT

Defy gravity—and convention—by spending some time in a mod 1960s Bubble Chair, originally designed by Eero Aarnio of Finland. If you prefer your décor more organic, you can opt for the Bohemian chic rattan version. Who says your feet need to be planted on the ground?

86

BUNNY HOP

Think cute has no place in modernism? Think again! Reinvent the classic English animal painting with bold lines and bright colors, as artist Hunt Slonem has done with his rabbit portraits. Above all, never take your home (or yourself) too seriously.

87 LOVE IS ALL YOU NEED

For all the advancements of the past several decades, we often feel more fractured than ever. For all our connectivity, it is easy to feel alone. Go forth with love in your heart. Donate to that charity you admire; accept that last-minute invitation; serve on that committee. Adopt a shelter animal—a pet will teach you the meaning of love, to be sure. Tell your family you love them, for life is precious and fleeting. Alone, we may not be able to change the world, but we can change our corner of it. We do so by spreading love, little by little, day by day. Choose love. Today.

For this love-filled den, I painted the walls a deep high-gloss teal for richness, complemented by pops of bright white and jet black, all accented with gold for a bit of shine.

88 BE OPTIMISTIC

After World War II, America experienced a natural high. We built suburbs; we had babies; we created gadgets. A few years later, John F. Kennedy announced that we would put a man on the moon. In short, we lived in a world of possibility. Our homes reflected that sense of unbridled optimism.

Come on, America, let's dream again! As Eleanor Roosevelt said, "The future belongs to those who believe in the beauty of their dreams."

I, for one, cannot wait to see what's next.

Anything could happen ♡

73451

89

STEEL YOURSELF

You don't need to have bar–barians at the gate to desire a formidable first impression. Many of the homes built for celebrities during the Palm Springs midcentury heyday featured an imposing front wall with few or no windows. Privacy aside, a little mystery goes a long way.

90
TREAD LIGHTLY

While a tradition that is more Canadian and Asian—removing your shoes when entering a home—has a ritualistic appeal and documented health benefits. I created an unexpected entry moment with a vintage shelving unit from the Pierre Cardin retail stores and a simple basket from Pottery Barn.

91 BOTTLE LOGIC

I have never been accused of over-accessorizing. That said, I do believe that "it's the small things," and that details give a room its soul.

So where to begin? Do you rush out to your nearest discount store and buy a bunch of cheap junk? I say no. Don't contribute to our disposable society.

Vintage bottles are one of my favorite accessories. They are easy to source online, at antique stores, or estate sales. They can be used alone, but in multiples they create a major statement. Try grouping numerous bottles of various shapes in your preferred accent color to add instant retro flair and a foolproof focal point.

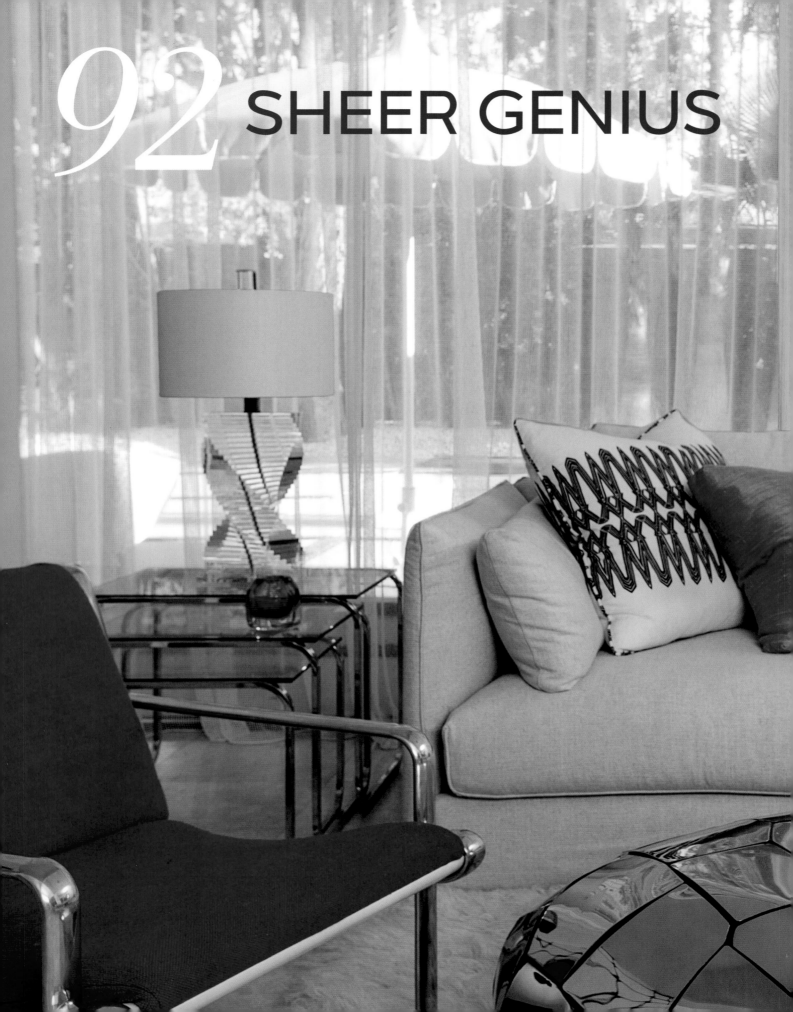

Many modern homeowners are hesitant to install draperies, and yet, fabric window treatments were standard fare in the 1950s and 1960s. I like to treat large windows with wall-to-wall, floor-to-ceiling draperies. They add a layer of warmth to a minimal interior. Draw them open to enjoy the view, or close them for a layer of privacy and softness.

93

CLEAR OUT

Originally created in the 1930s by DuPont under the brand name Lucite, acrylic resin was quickly adopted for a variety of decorative uses, including handbags, jewelry, and furniture. In World War II, acrylic was widely used for military applications including submarine periscopes and airplane windshields. After the war, acrylic manufacturers needed to find commercial uses for the material, and in the following decades, Lucite furniture had its heyday.

94 MAKE DO

Don't have high ceilings? Don't worry. Our modernist forebearers never hesitated to swag a chandelier when necessary. When my client did not have tall ceilings to hang the chandelier she loved, I chose to place it in an otherwise unused corner and allow it to dangle danger-ously low to the ground. We created an instant focal point from both inside and out. Midcentury designers were continual problem-solvers; be part of that tradition.

95 CATCH THE BREEZE

When I want to add some midcentury modern verve to an unremarkable structure, I go back to the building blocks. More specifically, to breeze blocks. Originally designed to shelter a building envelope from the sun, these midcentury workhorses were ubiquitous well into the 1970s (even gracing my college dormitory) before falling out of favor. Now they are back and better than ever.

I added a breeze block wall to this project in Palm Desert, creating privacy for a bedroom patio and a dramatic backdrop for outdoor dining.

96 GROW YOUR GARDEN

White picket fences. A patch of dirt to call your own. It is all part of the American Dream. Nourish your inner homestead tendencies by planting something in the ground. Herbs or vegetables are especially useful. Even if you live in an apartment, a potted garden brings joy and connection to the earth. Plant. Nurture. Watch it grow.

97 BUCKLE UP

We honor the past by looking to the future. If the great midcentury creators were alive today, they would not be resting on their laurels. They would not be imitating. They would be pushing design forward. Much like these dining chairs do. Designed by my friends at The Phillips Collection, they take the classic Verner Panton shape and reimagine it with—that's right—recycled seat belts. Hold onto your hats, modernists: the future looks bright.

98
FIND MEANING

Part of modernism, for me, is surrounding oneself with fewer things, but things that have meaning. Proudly display your collections, even in the most unlikely of places. Wear your heart on your sleeve. Show the world who and what you are—or what you strive to be.

99 SLEEP SOFTLY

It is relatively easy to find midcentury bedroom sets online, at your local flea market, or at a vintage store. Though I rarely want a matched set, the pieces are normally sold together and are even less expensive when bought this way.

I will incorporate the nightstands and dresser into my bedroom designs (sometimes in different rooms), but the vintage beds are inevitably too small for our modern mattresses and sleeping habits. This is why so many of my bedroom designs incorporate fabric beds and headboards—they are easy to make and then there is no worry about matching the vintage wood finish, and really, isn't it so much cozier? And much less matchy-matchy.

100 PEACE OUT

For me, design is about joy. It is about creating places and products that put a smile on your face. It is about a bedroom that inspires you when you open your eyes; a living room that embraces you after a long day. It is about a respite from the busyness of the world. If I have put a smile on your face, I consider it a job well done.

ACKNOWLEDGMENTS

To me, "thank" and "you"—used together—are the most magical words on Earth. They have amazing healing and creative power.

And yet, *thank you* does not seem adequate to express my feelings for all the people that make my business, and this book, possible.

To my parents: Our time together on this earth was far too brief, but our time together is just beginning. I thank you for the countless gifts you have given me and I strive each day to honor your legacy. And to my other parents, who opened their hearts and lives to me, and who left their indelible mark: Lee Seebach and Lydia Troth—thank you.

To my husband, David Clark: Thank you for giving me the freedom to pursue my passion and for being at my side, as my "hobby" has become our profession.

Many colleagues, past and present, have made Christopher Kennedy, Inc. what it is today and my gratitude knows no bounds. John-Patrick Flynn and Francie Flynn: Thank you for the creativity, loyalty, and acumen that built this company brick by brick. Felix Barthelemy, your dedication and good nature made the trains run on time, pleasantly, for so many years. And to the other talented compatriots who have loaned their time and talents to the cause, I thank you: Ben Lizardi, Chris Kjos, Jim Cook, Paul and Giacomina Palodichuk, Penelope Francis, Laura Svolos, Jennifer Beckley Sides, Clint Thorne, Debbie Anderson, Haley Jeanne Freckleton, Ashley Sobeck, Ann-Britt Holm, Tobby Llora, James Patton, Rosemary Seidner, Vanessa Kogevinas, Minh Tran, and the team at A & J's Deliveries.

To Keith Fortner, Senior Designer with our company: Your talent styled these pages and your friendship keeps me going. Thank you for your camaraderie, good taste, tough love, and hard work.

Thank you to my many clients, many of whom saw the seeds of possibility early on, and have become champions, mentors, and friends. The beautiful images on these pages are first and foremost your homes, and I thank you for sharing them with the world, allowing us all into your private worlds so that we may swoon and dream.

Thank you to Gibbs for believing in me, and to the team at Gibbs Smith for bringing my idea to life: editor Katie Killebrew and designer Sheryl Dickert.

Thank you to Gretchen Aubuchon and Brendan Von Enck for being my agents, champions, and most importantly, friends.

Finally, thank you to the one person whom I cannot remember life without: J. Rockwell Seebach—first friend, then stepbrother, and now brother always. Thank you for always having my back. The time spent creating this book together is the best gift of all, and it is certainly as much yours as it is mine.